Alexander N. Scriabin

Selected Piano Pieces
Ausgewählte Klavierstücke

F 95088

ROB. FORBERG MUSIKVERLAG

INDEX · INHALT

© 2019 Rob. Forberg Musikverlag, Berlin (for all countries · für alle Länder)

F 95088

ISMN 979-0-2061-0622-4

INTRODUCTION

This edition encompasses different styles and genres found in the piano works of Alexander Scriabin (1872-1915). Some of these genres would generate full-bodied collections, which would follow the composer's artistic itinerary every step of the way: such is the case of the ten *Sonatas*, a cycle in which Scriabin's poetic tendencies are fully expressed, as well as in the twenty *Poèmes*. From 1903 on, when Scriabin first decided that the term "poème" could be used as title of a piece, they would always remain in his catalogue, at times as individual pieces or as thematic collections, at other times in combination with works with different titles.

The waltz is one of the least explored genres by Scriabin. He would compose five: three in 1886, one of which is the op. 1 published here, and two others without opus numbers. In the 1886 juvenile *Valses* (we should remember that, at the time, Scriabin was just fourteen years old) Chopin's influence is conspicuous, and the prevailing tone is one of seductive grace, at times veiled with melancholy. The *Valse* in F minor op. 1 is the one that best foreshadows the future developments of Scriabin's style, by virtue of a secondary episode in which emotions burst out irrepressibly and the harmony becomes ambiguous. The *Valses* of 1886, whose style is still reminiscent of waltzes for actual dancing, would be followed, almost twenty years later, by the *Valse* op. 38, with its convulsive and passionate movements, and a *Quasi valse* op. 47 in which Scriabin seems to want to make this form, which is only slightly hinted at, evaporate definitively.

In contrast, to the *étude* genre Scriabin dedicated two ample collections (op. 8 and op. 42), which were followed by two brief pages in miscellaneous collections (op. 49 No. 1 and op. 56 No. 4) and op. 65, a triptych from his later period. This path began with the brief *Étude* published here, op. 2 No. 1 in C-sharp minor (1887), which would gain widespread recognition: this intensely compelling work was part of, among others, Vladimir Horowitz's repertoire, who frequently included it in his programs (it was one of the encores of his legendary return concert of 1965).

The most extensive piece in this collection is the youthful *Sonata-Fantaisie* in G-sharp minor (composed in 1886, the same year as the *Valse*), not to be confused with the more widely-known second *Sonata* op. 19 (1892-97) in the same key, equally structured in two linked movements and called *Sonata-Fantaisie* as well. The 1886 *Sonata-Fantaisie* is one of the stages in Scriabin's journey towards his official sonata cycle: next to it, there is also the *Sonata* in E-flat minor written between 1887 and 1889, whose first movement served as a base for the *Allegro appassionato* op. 4. The two movements that make up the 1886 *Sonata-Fantaisie*, as opposed to those found in the second *Sonata*, are not uniform in weight and function: the first, briefer and less articulate than the second, serves as an introduction, while the second displays a clear sonata form (complete with repeat signs at the end of the exposition, a feature that Scriabin would also use in his first *Sonata* op. 6). At the end of the second movement, the piece falls back on a melancholy citation drawn from the opening Andante. Regarding these features, this juvenile *Sonata-Fantaisie* demonstrates an affinity not with the second, but with the fourth *Sonata* op. 30 written almost twenty years later (1903), in which, however, the closing quote of the introduction boasts an opposite character: jubilant and ecstatic.

Finally, we arrive at the last period of Scriabin's artistic production, with the *Poème* op. 71 No. 1 (1914), the first of the two in the collection. As far as the *poème* genre is concerned, the only other one to follow it would be the renowned *Vers la flamme* op. 72, composed during the same year. Its opening indication is "Fantastique". Here, as on many other occasions, Scriabin explores the aphoristic form and, in a few meteoric bars, brings together extremely pronounced gestures: asking questions, climaxing temporarily, casting a veil of mystery and evaporating into nothing. A glimpse of ecstasy, or rather, of the road that leads towards its infinite pursuit.

Alfonso Alberti
(translation by Avery Gosfield)

EINLEITUNG

Die vorliegende Edition stellt Klavierkompositionen von Alexander Skrjabin (1872–1915) vor, die verschiedenen Stilen und Gattungen angehören. Einige davon stammen aus umfangreichen Sammlungen, in denen sich Skrjabins kompositorische Entwicklung Schritt für Schritt nachvollziehen lässt. Das gilt etwa für die zehn Sonaten, einen Zyklus, in dem die Skrjabin'sche Ästhetik sich in ihrer ganzen Vollendung zeigt, aber auch für die zwanzig Werke, die den Titel *Poèmes* tragen. 1903 entschied sich Skrjabin zum ersten Mal, eines seiner Werke „poème" zu nennen (also „Gedicht"), und danach hat er diesen Titel in seinem Œuvre immer wieder verwendet, sei es für Einzelwerke oder für Sammlungen mit diesem Titel oder auch in Zusammenstellungen mit weiteren, anders betitelten Stücken.

Der Walzer ist eine Gattung, die Skrjabin eher selten ausgelotet hat. Er hat fünf komponiert: drei im Jahr 1886, von denen einer das hier abgedruckte op. 1 ist, und zwei weitere ohne Opusnummer. In diesen frühen Kompositionen (es sei daran erinnert, dass Skrjabin ja erst 14 Jahre zählte) ist der Einfluss von Chopin überdeutlich, und der vorherrschende Ton ist der einer verführerischen Anmut, manchmal einer verhangenen Melancholie. Der *Valse* in f-Moll op. 1 ist derjenige, in dem ein Nebenthema mit einem emotionalen Ausbruch und einer kühneren Harmonie am deutlichsten die zukünftigen Entwicklungen von Skrjabins Stil ahnen lässt. Den Walzern aus dem Jahr 1886, die wirklich noch „tanzbar" sind, folgen nahezu zwanzig Jahre später der *Valse* op. 38 mit seinen exzessiven und leidenschaftlichen Bewegungen und der *Quasi valse* op. 47, in dem Skrjabin scheinbar daran geht, die nur kurz angedeutete Form aufzulösen.

Der Gattung Etüde widmete Skrjabin hingegen zwei umfangreiche Sammlungen (op. 8 und op. 42), gefolgt von zwei kurzen Kompositionen in gemischten Sammlungen (op. 49 Nr. 1 und op. 56 Nr. 4) und den drei *Etüden* op. 65. Am Beginn steht die hier vorgestellte kurze *Étude* op. 2 Nr. 1 in cis-Moll (1887), die sehr berühmt werden sollte: Dieses überaus reizvolle Werk gehörte unter anderem zum Repertoire von Vladimir Horowitz, der es oft in seinen Konzerten spielte (es war auch eine der Zugaben bei seiner legendären Rückkehr auf das Podium im Jahr 1965).

Das umfangreichste Stück der vorliegenden Auswahl ist die frühe *Sonate-Fantaisie* in gis-Moll (sie entstand 1886, im selben Jahr wie der *Valse*), nicht zu verwechseln mit der berühmteren, in derselben Tonart gehaltenen zweiten *Sonate* op. 19 (1892–97) die wie die frühe aus zwei aufeinander bezogenen Sätzen besteht und ebenfalls unter dem Titel *Sonate-Fantaisie* bekannt ist. Die frühe *Sonate* ist eine Station auf Skrjabins Weg zum offiziellen Zyklus seiner Sonaten; außerdem komponierte er zwischen 1887 und 1889 noch eine *Sonate* in es-Moll, deren erster Satz zum *Allegro appassionato* op. 4 wurde. Anders als bei der zweiten *Sonate* sind die beiden Sätze der frühen *Sonate-Fantaisie* aus dem Jahr 1886 weder von der Bedeutung noch von der Funktion her homogen: Der erste Satz, kürzer und weniger artikuliert, übernimmt die Funktion einer Einleitung, während der zweite eindeutig in der Sonatensatzform gehalten ist (inklusive der Angabe zur Wiederholung der Exposition, wie sie Skrjabin später auch in der ersten *Sonate* op. 6 noch vorschreibt). Am Ende des zweiten Satzes kehrt das Stück mit einem wehmütigen Zitat wieder zum Andante des Anfangs zurück. Damit erweist sich die frühe *Sonate-Fantaisie* als nicht mit der zweiten, sondern mit der fast zwanzig Jahre später entstandenen vierten *Sonate* op. 30 (1903) verwandt, in der allerdings das abschließende Zitat der Einleitung von entgegengesetztem Charakter ist: jubelnd und ekstatisch.

Die letzte Periode im Schaffen von Skrjabin ist mit den *Poèmes* op. 71 (1914) erreicht, von denen hier die Nr. 1 abgedruckt ist. In der Gattung des Poems folgte danach nur noch das berühmte *Vers la flamme* op. 72, das im selben Jahr entstand. „Fantastique" lautet die erste Spielanweisung. Skrjabin erkundet hier wie so oft die aphoristische Form, und in wenigen rasanten Takten reiht er Gesten von extremer Deutlichkeit aneinander: Verlangendes Fragen führt zu einem vorläufigen Höhepunkt, eine weitere Episode zeigt sich geheimnisvoll, die letzte verflüchtigt sich. Es ist das Fragment einer Ekstase, oder besser gesagt: Fragmente des Wegs auf der unendlichen Suche nach ihr.

Alfonso Alberti
(Übersetzung Birgit Gotzes)

Sonate-Fantaisie

Alexander N. Scriabin (1871-1915)
1886

Klavier

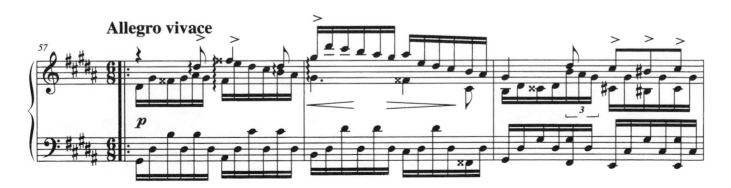

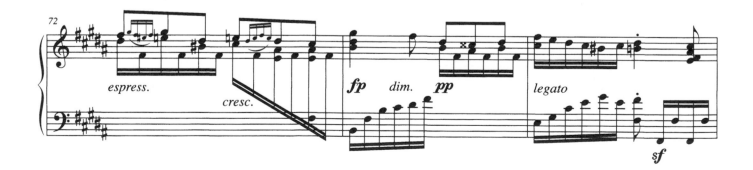

un poco meno vivo

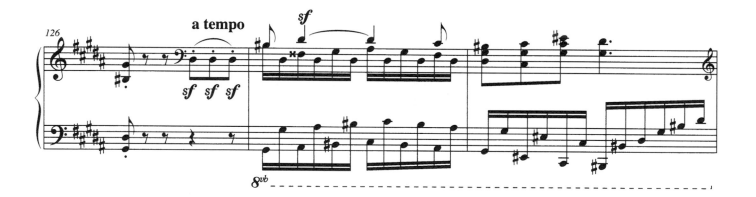

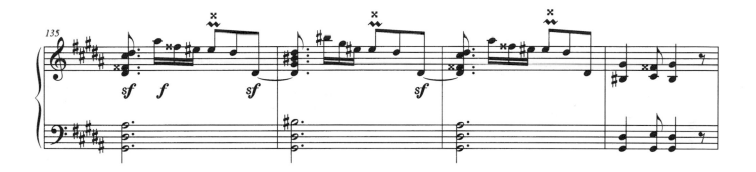

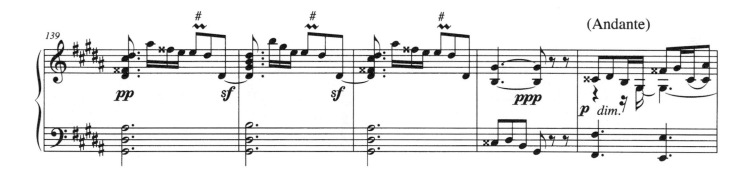

Valse op. 1

1886

Klavier

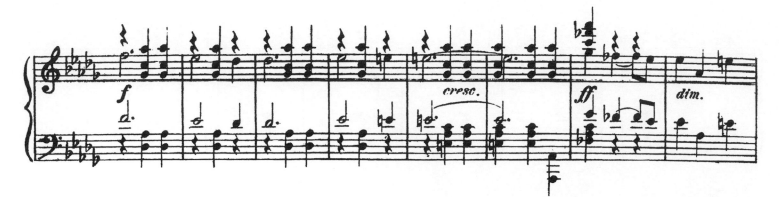

Étude op. 2 No. 1

1887

Klavier

Poème op. 71 No. 1

1914

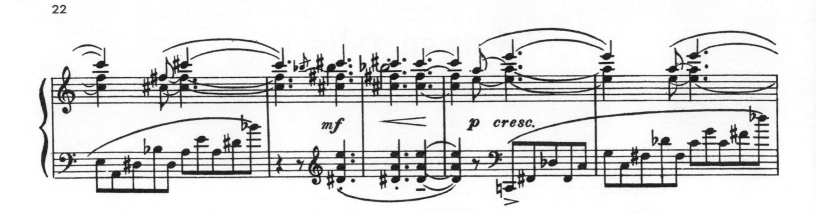

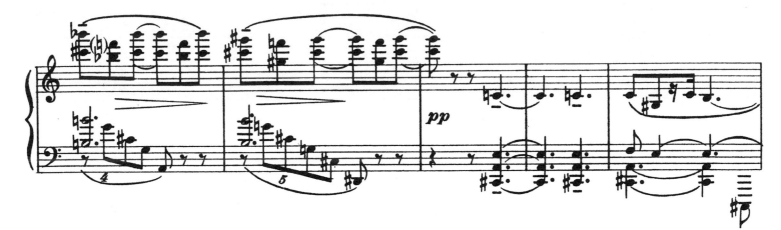

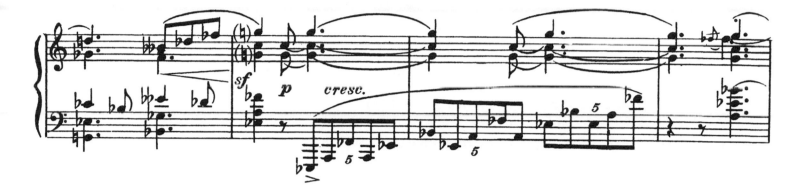

Russian Piano Music · Russische Klaviermusik

Russian Piano Collection (F 95030)
The big book of Russian piano music from Glinka to Prokofiev
Das große Buch der russischen Klaviermusik von Glinka bis Prokofjew

Russian Album for Piano (F 95042)
13 Easy to intermediate level piano pieces by Moussorgsky, Tchaikovsky and others
13 leichte bis mittelschwere Klavierstücke von Mussorgsky, Tschaikowsky und anderen

Russian Music for Young Pianists (F 95076)
15 Easy level piano pieces by Prokofieff, Tchaikovsky and others
15 leichte Klavierstücke von Prokofjew, Tschaikowsky und anderen

Russian Piano Collection for Four Hands (F 95075)
14 Intermediate level piano pieces by Arensky, Balakirew and others
14 mittelschwere Klavierstücke von Arensky, Balakirew und anderen

Pyotr I. Tchaikovsky
· The Swan Lake Suite and The Nutcracker Suite (F 95057)
· Album for Piano (F 95058)
 12 Intermediate level piano pieces · 12 mittelschwere Klavierstücke
· Piano Collection (F 95073)
 28 Intermediate level piano pieces · 28 mittelschwere Klavierstücke

Vladimir Rebikov: 15 Piano Pieces (F 95053)
15 Easy to intermediate level piano pieces · 15 leichte bis mittelschwere Klavierstücke

Sergei Prokofiev
· Selected Pieces and Studies (F 95071)
 22 Intermediate level piano pieces and studies · 22 mittelschwere Klavierstücke und Etüden
· Four pieces op. 3 (F 95069)
· Four pieces op. 4 (F 95070)

Modest Mussorgsky: Selected Piano Pieces (F 95072)
11 Intermediate level piano pieces · 11 mittelschwere Klavierstücke

Anton S. Arensky: Twelve Preludes for Piano op. 63 (F 95077)

Eduard F. Nápravník: Deux pièces espagnoles for Piano op. 51 (F 95083)

Alexander N. Scriabin
· Three Studies op. 65 (F 95078)
· Impromptus à la mazur op. 7 (F 95079)
· Three Sonatas op. 66, 68, 70 (F 95080)